THE EARTH GODS

The Books of

KAHLIL GIBRAN

"His power came from some great reservoir of spiritual life else it could not have been so universal and so potent, but the majesty and beauty of the language with which he clothed it were all his own." — CLAUDE BRAGDON

The Madman · 1918

Twenty Drawings · 1919

The Forerunner · 1920

The Prophet · 1923

Sand and Foam · 1926

Jesus the Son of Man · 1928

The Earth Gods · 1931

The Wanderer · 1932

The Garden of the Prophet · 1933

Prose Poems · 1934

Nymphs of the Valley · 1948

Spirits Rebellious · 1948

A Tear and a Smile · 1950

∴

This Man from Lebanon —

A Study of Kahlil Gibran
by Barbara Young

PUBLISHED BY ALFRED A. KNOPF

THE
EARTH GODS

BY

Kahlil Gibran

1969

NEW YORK : ALFRED·A·KNOPF

THIS IS A BORZOI BOOK,
PUBLISHED BY ALFRED A. KNOPF, INC.

FIFTEENTH PRINTING

*The twelve illustrations in this volume
are reproduced from original drawings
by the author*

THE EARTH GODS

WHEN the night of the twelfth æon fell,
And silence, the high tide of night, swallowed the
hills,
The three earth-born gods, the Master Titans of
life,
Appeared upon the mountains.

Rivers ran about their feet;
The mist floated across their breasts,
And their heads rose in majesty above the world.

Then they spoke, and like distant thunder
Their voices rolled over the plains.

3

FIRST GOD

The wind blows eastward;
I would turn my face to the south,
For the wind crowds my nostrils with the odors of
　　dead things.

SECOND GOD

It is the scent of burnt flesh, sweet and bountiful.
I would breathe it.

FIRST GOD

It is the odor of mortality parching upon its own
　　faint flame.
Heavily does it hang upon the air,
And like foul breath of the pit
It offends my senses.
I would turn my face to the scentless north.

SECOND GOD

It is the inflamed fragrance of brooding life
4

That I would breathe now and forever.
Gods live upon sacrifice,
Their thirst quenched by blood,
Their hearts appeased with young souls,
Their sinews strengthened by the deathless sighs
Of those who dwell with death;
Their thrones are built upon the ashes of genera-
tions.

FIRST GOD

Weary is my spirit of all there is.
I would not move a hand to create a world
Nor to erase one.

I would not live could I but die,
For the weight of æons is upon me,
And the ceaseless moan of the seas exhausts my
sleep.
Could I but lose the primal aim
And vanish like a wasted sun;
Could I but strip my divinity of its purpose

And breathe my immortality into space,
And be no more;
Could I but be consumed and pass from time's memory
Into the emptiness of nowhere!

Listen my brothers, my ancient brothers.
A youth in yonder vale
Is singing his heart to the night.
His lyre is gold and ebony.
His voice is silver and gold.

I would not be so vain as to be no more.
I could not but choose the hardest way;
To follow the seasons and support the majesty of
    the years;
To sow the seed and to watch it thrust through the
    soil;
To call the flower from its hiding place
6

And give it strength to nestle its own life,
And then to pluck it when the storm laughs in the
    forest;
To raise man from secret darkness,
Yet keep his roots clinging to the earth;
To give him thirst for life, and make death his cup-
    bearer;
To endow him with love that waxeth with pain,
And exalts with desire, and increases with longing,
And fadeth away with the first embrace;
To girdle his nights with dreams of higher days,
And infuse his days with visions of blissful nights,
And yet to confine his days and his nights
To their immutable resemblance;
To make his fancy like the eagle of the mountain,
And his thought as the tempests of the seas,
And yet to give him hands slow in decision,
And feet heavy with deliberation;
To give him gladness that he may sing before us,
And sorrow that he may call unto us,
And then to lay him low,

When the earth in her hunger cries for food;
To raise his soul high above the firmament
That he may foretaste our tomorrow,
And to keep his body groveling in the mire
That he may not forget his yesterday.

Thus shall we rule man unto the end of time,
Governing the breath that began with his mother's
    crying,
And ends with the lamentation of his children.

FIRST GOD

My heart thirsts, yet I would not drink the faint
    blood of a feeble race,
For the cup is tainted, and the vintage therein is
    bitter to my mouth.
Like thee I have kneaded the clay and fashioned it
    to breathing forms
That crept out of my dripping fingers unto the
    marshes and the hills.

8

Like thee I have kindled the dark depths of begin-
ning life
And watched it crawl from caves to rocky heights.
Like thee I have summoned spring and laid the
beauty thereof
For a lure that seizes youth and binds it to generate
and multiply.
Like thee I have led man from shrine to shrine,
And turned his mute fear of things unseen
To tremulous faith in us, the unvisited and the un-
known.
Like thee I have ridden the wild tempest over his
head
That he might bow before us,
And shaken the earth beneath him until he cried
unto us;
And like thee, led the savage ocean against his
nested isle,
Till he hath died calling upon us.
All this have I done, and more.
And all that I have done is empty and vain.

9

Vain is the waking and empty is the sleep,
And thrice empty and vain is the dream.

THIRD GOD

Brothers, my august brothers,
Down in the myrtle grove
A girl is dancing to the moon,
A thousand dew-stars are in her hair,
About her feet a thousand wings.

SECOND GOD

We have planted man, our vine, and tilled the soil
In the purple mist of the first dawn.
We watched the lean branches grow,
And through the days of seasonless years
We nursed the infant leaves.
From the angry element we shielded the bud,
And against all dark spirits we guarded the flower.
And now that our vine hath yielded the grape
You will not take it to the winepress and fill the
    cup.

Whose mightier hand than yours shall reap the
fruit?

And what nobler end than your thirst awaits the
wine?

Man is food for the gods,

And the glory of man begins

When his aimless breath is sucked by gods' hal-
lowed lips.

All that is human counts for naught if human it re-
main;

The innocence of childhood, and the sweet ecstasy
of youth,

The passion of stern manhood, and the wisdom of
old age;

The splendor of kings and the triumph of warriors,

The fame of poets and the honor of dreamers and
saints;

All these and all that lieth therein is bred for gods.

And naught but bread ungraced shall it be

If the gods raise it not to their mouths.

And as the mute grain turns to love songs when

swallowed by the nightingale,

Even so as bread for gods shall man taste godhead.

Aye, man is meat for gods!

And all that is man shall come upon the gods' eternal board!

The pain of child-bearing and the agony of childbirth,

The blind cry of the infant that pierces the naked night,

And the anguish of the mother wrestling with the sleep she craves,

To pour life exhausted from her breast;

The flaming breath of youth tormented,

And the burdened sobs of passion unspent;

The dripping brows of manhood tilling the barren land,

And the regret of pale old age when life against life's will

Calls to the grave.

12

Behold this is man!
A creature bred on hunger and made food for hun-
    gry gods.
A vine that creeps in dust beneath the feet of death-
    less death.
The flower that blooms in nights of evil shadows;
The grape of mournful days, and days of terror and
    shame.
And yet you would have me eat and drink.
You would bid me sit amongst shrouded faces
And draw my life from stony lips
And from withered hands receive my eternity.

THIRD GOD

Brothers, my dreaded brothers,
Thrice deep the youth is singing,
And thrice higher is his song.
His voice shakes the forest
And pierces the sky,
And scatters the slumbering of earth.

13

SECOND GOD *(Always unhearing)*

The bee hums harshly in your ears,
And foul is the honey to your lips.
Fain would I comfort you,
But how shall I?
Only the abyss listens when gods call unto gods,
For measureless is the gulf that lies between divini-
    ties,
And windless is the space.
Yet I would comfort you,
I would make serene your clouded sphere;
And though equal we are in power and judgment,
I would counsel you.

When out of chaos came the earth, and we, sons
of the beginning, beheld each other in the lustless
light, we breathed the first hushed, tremulous sound
that quickened the currents of air and sea.

Then we walked, hand in hand, upon the gray infant world, and out of the echoes of our first drowsy
steps time was born, a fourth divinity, that sets his

feet upon our footprints, shadowing our thoughts and desires, and seeing only with our eyes.

And unto earth came life, and unto life came the spirit, the winged melody of the universe. And we ruled life and spirit, and none save us knew the measure of the years nor the weight of years' nebulous dreams, till we, at noontide of the seventh æon, gave the sea in marriage to the sun.

And from the inner chamber of their nuptial ecstasy, we brought man, a creature who, though yielding and infirm, bears ever the marks of his parentage.

Through man who walks earth with eyes upon the stars, we find pathways to earth's distant regions; and of man, the humble reed growing beside dark waters, we make a flute through whose hollowed heart we pour our voice to the silence-bound world.
From the sunless north to the sun-smitten sand of
    the south.
From the lotus land where days are born
To perilous isles where days are slain,

Man, the faint hearted, overbold by our purpose,
Ventures with lyre and sword.
Ours is the will he heralds,
And our the sovereignty he proclaims,
And his love trodden courses are rivers, to the sea of
    our desires.
We, upon the heights, in man's sleep dream our
    dreams.
We urge his days to part from the valley of twilights
And seek their fullness upon the hills.
Our hands direct the tempests that sweep the world
And summon man from sterile peace to fertile strife,
And on to triumph.
In our eyes is the vision that turns man's soul to
    flame,
And leads him to exalted loneliness and rebellious
    prophecy,
And on to crucifixion.
Man is born to bondage,
And in bondage is his honor and his reward.
In man we seek a mouthpiece,

And in his life our self fulfillment.
Whose heart shall echo our voice if the human heart
  is deafened with dust?
Who shall behold our shining if man's eye is blinded
  with night?
And what would you do with man, child of our
  earliest heart, our own self image?

THIRD GOD

Brothers, my mighty brothers,
The dancer's feet are drunk with songs.
They set the air a-throbbing,
And like doves her hands fly upward.

FIRST GOD

The lark calls to the lark,
But upward the eagle soars,
Nor tarries to hear the song.
You would teach me self love fulfilled in man's
  worship,
And content with man's servitude.

But my self love is limitless and without measure.
I would rise beyond my earthbound mortality
And throne me upon the heavens.
My arms would girdle space and encompass the
    spheres.
I would take the starry way for a bow,
And the comets for arrows,
And with the infinite would I conquer the infinite.

But you would not do this, were it in your power.
For even as man is to man,
So are gods to gods.
Nay, you would bring to my weary heart
Remembrance of cycles spent in mist,
When my soul sought itself among the mountains
And mine eyes pursued their own image in slumber-
    ing waters;
Though my yesterday died in child-birth
And only silence visits her womb,
And the wind strewn sand nestles at her breast.
18

Oh yesterday, dead yesterday,
Mother of my chained divinity,
What super-god caught you in your flight
And made you breed in the cage?
What giant sun warmed your bosom
To give me birth?
I bless you not, yet I would not curse you;
For even as you have burdened me with life
So I have burdened man.
But less cruel have I been.
I, immortal, made man a passing shadow;
And you, dying, conceived me deathless.

Yesterday, dead yesterday,
Shall you return with distant tomorrow,
That I may bring you to judgment?
And will you wake with life's second dawn
That I may erase your earth-clinging memory from
    the earth?
Would that you might rise with all the dead of yore,
Till the land choke with its own bitter fruit,

And all the seas be stagnant with the slain,
And woe upon woe exhaust earth's vain fertility.

THIRD GOD

Brother, my sacred brothers,
The girl has heard the song,
And now she seeks the singer.
Like a fawn in glad surprise
She leaps over rocks and streams
And turns her to every side.
Oh, the joy in mortal intent,
The eye of purpose half-born;
The smile on lips that quiver
With foretaste of promised delight!
What flower has fallen from heaven,
What flame has risen from hell,
That startled the heart of silence
To this breathless joy and fear?
What dream dreamt we upon the height,
What thought gave we to the wind
That woke the drowsing valley
And made watchful the night?

20

SECOND GOD

The sacred loom is given you,
And the art to weave the fabric.
The loom and the art shall be yours forevermore,
And yours the dark thread and the light,
And yours the purple and the gold.
Yet you would grudge yourself a raiment.
Your hands have spun man's soul
From living air and fire,
Yet now you would break the thread,
And lend your versèd fingers to an idle eternity.

FIRST GOD

Nay, unto eternity unmoulded I would give my
    hands,
And to untrodden fields assign my feet.
What joy is there in songs oft heard,
Whose tune the remembering ear arrests
Ere the breath yields it to the wind?
My heart longs for what my heart conceives not,

And unto the unknown where memory dwells not
I would command my spirit.
Oh, tempt me not with glory possessed,
And seek not to comfort me with your dream or
mine,
For all that I am, and all that there is on earth,
And all that shall be, inviteth not my soul.
Oh my soul,
Silent is thy face,
And in thine eyes the shadows of night are sleep-
ing.
But terrible is thy silence,
And thou art terrible.

THIRD GOD

Brothers, my solemn brothers,
The girl has found the singer.
She sees his raptured face.
Panther-like she slips with subtle steps
Through rustling vine and fern.
And now amid his ardent cries
22

He gazes full on her.

Oh my brothers, my heedless brothers,
Is it some other god in passion
Who has woven this web of scarlet and white?
What unbridled star has gone astray?
Whose secret keepeth night from morning?
And whose hand is upon our world?

FIRST GOD

Oh my soul, my soul,
Thou burning sphere that girdles me,
How shall I guide thy course,
And unto what space direct thy eagerness?

Oh my mateless soul,
In thy hunger thou preyest upon thyself,
And with thine own tears thou wouldst quench thy
      thirst;
For night gathers not her dew into thy cup,
And the day brings thee no fruit.

23

Oh my soul, my soul,
Thou grounded ship laden with desire,
Whence shall come the wind to fill thy sail,
And what higher tide shall release thy rudder?
Weighed is thine anchor and thy wings would
    spread,
But the skies are silent above thee,
And the still sea mocks at thy immobility.

And what hope is there for thee and me?
What shifting of worlds, what new purpose in the
    heavens,
That shall claim thee?
Does the womb of the virgin infinite
Bear the seed of thy Redeemer,
One mightier than thy vision
Whose hand shall deliver thee from thy captivity?

SECOND GOD

Hold your importunate cry,
And the breath of your burning heart,

For deaf is the ear of the infinite,
And heedless is the sky.
We are the beyond and we are the Most High,
And between us and boundless eternity
Is naught save our unshaped passion
And the motive thereof.

You invoke the unknown,
And the unknown clad with moving mist
Dwells in your own soul.
Yea, in your own soul your Redeemer lies asleep,
And in sleep sees what your waking eye does not see.
And that is the secret of our being.
Would you leave the harvest ungathered,
In haste to sow again the dreaming furrow?
And wherefore spread you your cloud in trackless
    fields and desolate,
When your own flock is seeking you,
And would fain gather in your shadow?
Forbear and look down upon the world.
Behold the unweaned children of your love.

The earth is your abode, and the earth is your
throne;
And high beyond man's furtherest hope
Your hand upholds his destiny.
You would not abandon him
Who strives to reach you through gladness and
through pain.
You would not turn away your face from the need
in his eye.

FIRST GOD

Does dawn hold the heart of night unto her heart?
Or shall the sea heed the bodies of her dead?
Like dawn my soul rises within me
Naked and unencumbered.
And like the unresting sea
My heart casts out a perishing wrack of man and
earth.
I would not cling to that that clings to me.
But unto that that rises beyond my reach I would
arise.

26

THIRD GOD

Brothers, behold, my brothers,
They meet, two star-bound spirits in the sky en-
    countering.
In silence they gaze the one upon the other.
He sings no more,
And yet his sunburnt throat throbs with the song;
And in her limbs the happy dance is stayed
But not asleep.

Brothers, my strange brothers,
The night waxeth deep,
And brighter is the moon,
And twixt the meadow and the sea
A voice in rapture calleth you and me.

SECOND GOD

To be, to rise, to burn before the burning sun,
To live, and to watch the nights of the living
As Orion watches us!

To face the four winds with a head crowned and
    high,
And to heal the ills of man with our tideless breath!
The tentmaker sits darkly at his loom,
And the potter turns his wheel unaware;
But we, the sleepless and the knowing,
We are released from guessing and from chance.
We pause not nor do we wait for thought.
We are beyond all restless questioning.
Be content and let the dreaming go.
Like rivers let us flow to ocean
Unwounded by the edges of the rocks;
And when we reach her heart and are merged,
No more shall we wrangle and reason of tomorrow.

FIRST GOD

Oh, this ache of ceaseless divining,
This vigil of guiding the day unto twilight,
And the night unto dawn;
This tide of ever remembering and forgetting;
This ever sowing destinies and reaping but hopes;

This changeless lifting of self from dust to mist,
Only to long for dust, and to fall down with long-
ing unto dust,
And still with greater longing to seek the mist again.
And this timeless measuring of time.
Must my soul needs to be a sea whose currents for-
ever confound one another,
Or the sky where the warring winds turn hurricane?

Were I man, a blind fragment,
I could have met it with patience.
Or if I were the Supreme Godhead,
Who fills the emptiness of man and of gods,
I would be fulfilled.
But you and I are neither human,
Nor the Supreme above us.
We are but twilights ever rising and ever fading
Between horizon and horizon.
We are but gods holding a world and held by it,
Fates that sound the trumpets
Whilst the breath and the music come from beyond.

29

And I rebel.

I would exhaust myself to emptiness.

I would dissolve myself afar from your vision,

And from the memory of this silent youth, our
younger brother,

Who sits beside us gazing into yonder valley,

And though his lips move, utters not a word.

THIRD GOD

I speak, my unheeding brothers,

I do indeed speak,

But you hear only your own words.

I bid you see your glory and mine,

But you turn, and close your eyes,

And rock your thrones.

Ye sovereigns who would govern the above world
and the world beneath,

Gods self-bent, whose yesterday is ever jealous of
your tomorrow,

Self-weary, who would unleash your temper with
speech

And lash our orb with thunderings!
Your feud is but the sounding of an Ancient Lyre
Whose strings have been half forgotten by His
    fingers
Who has Orion for a harp and the Pleiades for
    cymbals.
Even now, while you are muttering and rumbling,
His harp rings, His cymbals clash,
And I beseech you hear His song.

Behold, man and woman,
Flame to flame,
In white ecstasy.
Roots that suck at the breast of purple earth,
Flame flowers at the breasts of the sky.
And we are the purple breast,
And we are the enduring sky.
Our soul, even the soul of life, your soul and mine,
Dwells this night in a throat enflamed,
And garments the body of a girl with beating waves.
Your sceptre cannot sway this destiny,

Your weariness is but ambition.
This and all is wiped away
In the passion of a man and a maid.

SECOND GOD

Yea, what of this love of man and woman?
See how the east wind dances with her dancing feet,
And the west wind rises singing with his song.
Behold our sacred purpose now enthroned,
In the yielding of a spirit that sings to a body that
dances.

FIRST GOD

I will not turn my eyes downward to the conceit of
earth,
Nor to her children in their slow agony that you call
love.
And what is love,
But the muffled drum and leads the long procession
of sweet uncertainty
To another slow agony?
I will not look downward.

32

What is there to behold
Save a man and a woman in the forest that grew to
     trap them
That they might renounce self
And parent creatures for our unborn tomorrow?

THIRD GOD

Oh, the affliction of knowing,
The starless veil of prying and questioning
Which we have laid upon the world;
And the challenge to human forbearance!
We would lay under a stone a waxen shape
And say, It is a thing of clay,
And in clay let it find its end.
We would hold in our hands a white flame
And say in our heart,
It is a fragment of ourselves returning,
A breath of our breath that had escaped,
And now haunts our hands and lips for more fra-
     grance.
Earth gods, my brothers,

High upon the mountain,
We are still earth-bound,
Through man desiring the golden hours of man's
    destiny.
Shall our wisdom ravish beauty from his eyes?
Shall our measures subdue his passion to stillness,
Or to our own passion?

What would your armies of reasoning
Where love encamps his host?
They who are conquered by love,
And upon whose bodies love's chariot ran
From sea to mountain
And again from mountain to the sea,
Stand even now in a shy half-embrace.
Petal unto petal they breathe the sacred perfume,
Soul to soul they find the soul of life,
And upon their eyelids lies a prayer
Unto you and unto me.
Love is a night bent down to a bower anointed,
A sky turned meadow, and all the stars to fireflies.

34

True it is, we are the beyond,
And we are the most high.
But love is beyond our questioning,
And love outsoars our song.

SECOND GOD

Seek you a distant orb,
And would not consider this star
Where your sinews are planted?
There is no centre in space
Save where self is wedded to self,
And beauty is the witness and the priest.
And see and behold beauty scattered about our feet,
And beauty filling our hands to shame our lips.
The most distant is the most near.
And where beauty is, there are all things.

Oh, lofty dreaming brother,
Return to us from time's dim borderland!
Unlace your feet from no-where and no-when,
And dwell with us in this security

Which your hand interwined with ours
Has builded stone upon stone.
Cast off your mantle of brooding,
And comrade us, masters of the young earth green
  and warm.

FIRST GOD

Eternal Altar! Wouldst thou indeed this night
A god for sacrifice?
Now then, I come, and coming I offer up
My passion and my pain.
Lo, there is the dancer, carved out of our ancient
  eagerness,
And the singer is crying mine own songs unto the
  wind.
And in that dancing and in that singing
A god is slain within me.
My god-heart within my human ribs
Shouts to my god-heart in mid-air.
The human pit that wearied me calls to divinity.

The beauty that we have sought from the begin-
   ning
Calls unto divinity.
I heed, and I have measured the call,
And now I yield.
Beauty is a path that leads to self self-slain.
Beat your strings.
I will to walk the path.
It stretches ever to another dawn.

THIRD GOD

Love triumphs.
The white and green of love beside a lake,
And the proud majesty of love in tower or balcony;
Love in a garden or in the desert untrodden,
Love is our lord and master.
It is not a wanton decay of the flesh,
Nor the crumbling of desire
When desire and self are wrestling;
Nor is it flesh that takes arms against the spirit.
Love rebels not.

37

It only leaves the trodden way of ancient destinies
　　for the sacred grove,
To sing and dance its secret to eternity.
Love is youth with chains broken,
Manhood made free from the sod,
And womanhood warmed by the flame
And shining with the light of heaven deeper than
　　our heaven.
Love is a distant laughter in the spirit.
It is a wild assault that hushes you to your awaken-
　　ing.
It is a new dawn upon the earth,
A day not yet achieved in your eyes or mine,
But already achieved in its own greater heart.

Brothers, my brothers,
The bride comes from the heart of dawn,
And the bridegroom from the sunset.
There is a wedding in the valley.
A day too vast for recording.

38

Thus has it been since the first morn
Discharged the plains to hill and vale,
And thus shall it be to the last even-tide.
Our roots have brought forth the dancing branches
    in the valley,
And we are the flowering of the song-scent that rises
    to the heights.
Immortal and mortal, twin rivers calling to the sea.
There is no emptiness between call and call,
But only in the ear.
Time maketh our listening more certain,
And giveth it more desire.
Only doubt in mortal hushes the sound.
We have outsoared the doubt.
Man is a child of our younger heart.
Man is god in slow arising;
And betwixt his joy and his pain
Lies our sleeping, and the dreaming thereof.

FIRST GOD

Let the singer cry, and let the dancer whirl her feet
And let me be content awhile.
Let my soul be serene this night.
Perchance I may drowse, and drowsing
Behold a brighter world
And creatures more starry supple to my mind.

THIRD GOD

Now I will rise and strip me of time and space,
And I will dance in that field untrodden,
And the dancer's feet will move with my feet;
And I will sing in that higher air,
And a human voice will throb within my voice.

We shall pass into the twilight;
Perchance to wake to the dawn of another world.
But love shall stay,
And his finger-marks shall not be erased.

The blessed forge burns,
40

The sparks rise, and each spark is a sun.
Better it is for us, and wiser,
To seek a shadowed nook and sleep in our earth
divinity,
And let love, human and frail, command the com-
ing day.

A NOTE ON THE AUTHOR

KAHLIL GIBRAN, poet, philosopher, and artist, was
born in 1883 into an affluent and musical Lebanese
family. He was a college student in Syria at the age
of fifteen, studied art in Paris at the Ecole des
Beaux Arts, and had visited America twice before
he came to New York to stay in 1912 and adopted
English as his literary language. He died in New
York City's Greenwich Village on April 10, 1931.

His drawings and paintings have been exhibited
in the great capitals of the world and were com-
pared by Auguste Rodin to the work of William
Blake. *The Prophet,* his most popular book, published in 1923, has been translated into more than
twenty languages, and has sold well over a million
copies in this country alone.

This book was set on the linotype in Original Old Style. Of the history of this type very little is known; in practically its present form, it has been used for many years for fine book and magazine work. Original Old Style possesses in a high degree those two qualities by which a book type must be judged: first, legibility, and second, the ability to impart a definite character to a page without intruding itself upon the reader's consciousness.

PRINTED BY HALLIDAY LITHOGRAPH CORPORATION, WEST HANOVER, MASS. BOUND BY THE BOOK PRESS, BRATTLEBORO, VERMONT